Red Book

Critical Thinking with Literature

Reading • Writing • Communicating

by

Dorothy Kauffman, Ph.D.

University of Maryland

ISBN 0-8454-2453-X
Copyright © 1992 The Continental Press, Inc.

CONTINENTAL PRESS
Elizabethtown, PA 17022

Contents

Credits

Cover Design and Art Direction: Kirchoff/Wohlberg, Inc.

Interior Design: Kevin Miller

Illustration: Pages 7, 15, 21, 22, 27, 44, 59, 63, 83, 97, V. Carlin Verreaux; Pages 8–11, Leonard Jenkins; Pages 16–19, Sanford Kossin; Pages 24–24, Don Madden; Pages 28–30, Marianne Sachs; Pages 35–38, Oki Han; Pages 45–47, Tom Leonard; Pages 52–55, Linda Graves; Page 60, Liz Callen; Pages 64–67, Steve Cieslawski; Pages 71–73, Donald Gates; Pages 78–79, Debbie DeSaiz; Pages 84–87, Sharon O'Neil; Pages 98–100, Julie Ecklund; Pages 105–108, Bill Morrison

Photography: Page 5, Robert E. Kauffman

Acknowledgments

Every effort has been made to trace the ownership of all copyrighted material and to secure the necessary permissions to reprint these selections. In the event of any question arising as to the use of any material, the editor and the publisher, while expressing regret for any inadvertent error, will be happy to make the necessary correction in future printings. Grateful acknowledgment is made to the following for permission to reprint the copyrighted material listed below:

Alesia by Eloise Greenfield. Excerpt reprinted by permission of Philomel Books from *Alesia* by Eloise Geenfield, text © 1981 by Eloise Greenfield and Alesia Revis.

Jimmy Takes Vanishing Lessons by Walter R. Brooks. Text copyright © 1950 by Walter R. Brooks. Reprinted by permission of Alfred A. Knopf, Inc.

"Aunt Sponge and Aunt Spiker" from JAMES AND THE GIANT PEACH by Roald Dahl. Copyright © 1961 by Roald Dahl. Copyright renewed 1989 by Roald Dahl. Reprinted by permission of Alfred A. Knopf, Inc.

Shoeshine Girl by Clyde Robert Bulla. Text copyright © 1975 by Clyde Robert Bulla. Reprinted by permission of Harper & Row, Publishers, Inc.

"Momotaro: Boy-of-the-Peach" from *The Dancing Kettle and Other Japanese Folk Tales* by Yoshiko Uchida. Copyright © 1949 by Yoshiko Uchida. Reprinted by permission of Yoshiko Uchida.

Fog Magic by Julia Sauer. Copyright 1943, renewed © 1971 by Julia L. Sauer. All rights reserved. Reprinted by permission of Viking Penguin Inc.

"The Creature in the Classroom" from *The Baby Uggs Are Hatching* by Jack Prelutsky. Copyright © 1982 by Jack Prelutsky. Reprinted by permission of Greenwillow Books, a division of William Morrow and Company, Inc.

The Night the Monster Came Out by Mary Calhoun. Text copyright © 1982 by Mary Calhoun. Reprinted by permission of William Morrow and Company, Inc.

"The Gangster in the Back Seat" by Maria Leach reprinted by permission of Philomel Books from *The Thing at the Foot of the Bed and Other Scary Tales* by Maria Leach. Copyright © 1959 by Maria Leach, copyright renewed © 1987 by Macdonald H. Leach. Reprinted by permission of The Putnam Publishing Group.

"Bill Cosby" from *Laugh It Up* by George Zanderbergen. Copyright © 1976 by Crestwood House, Inc. Reprinted by permission of Crestwood House, Inc.

Charlotte's Web by E.B. White. Text copyright © 1952 by E.B. White. Text copyright renewed © 1980 by E.B. White. Reprinted by permission of Harper & Row, Publishers, Inc.

Garfield Bigger Than Life: His Third Book by Jim Davis. Copyright © 1981 by United Feature Syndicate, Inc. Reprinted by permission of United Feature Syndicate, Inc.

How to Eat Fried Worms by Thomas Rockwell. Copyright © 1973 by Franklin Watts, Inc. Reprinted by permission of Franklin Watts, Inc.

Dear Friend,

Because you read the title and looked at the cover of this book, you probably think it's a reading book. Well, you're right!

In this book, you will find a lot of different stories and some activities to do after you are done reading. When I chose the stories, I tried to find kinds of writing that kids I know would find interesting and fun to read. When I wrote the activities, I tried to find ways to help you think about the story. I know that sometimes after you read a story, you just fill in the blanks and close the book. I don't want that to happen here, so I talk to you in some of the activities. Sometimes I give you clues and ideas. Other times I even do a little part for you. This way, you and I can work together.

By now, you might be wondering what kind of person wrote this book. I like to do a lot of things. I like to read and write. I like to cook, but I hate to clean up. I like to go barefoot, and I like to wear boots. And if I don't like doing something, I put it off till it can't wait any longer. These are just a few things that tell the kind of person I am. Now here's a picture of me and my two cats to show you what I look like.

Happy reading,

Dotti

KIDS LIKE ME

Who is your best friend? Why do you say this person is your best friend?

_____

_____

_____

People often choose friends who are very much like themselves. Think about the best friend you talked about above. How are you and your friend alike? List some ways here.

```
_____          _____
_____  HOW MY  _____
_____ FRIEND AND I _____
_____ ARE ALIKE _____
_____          _____
```

Now read these sentences. Put a check beside the ones that tell how you and your friend are alike.

_____ **1.** We do a lot of things we are supposed to do without being told.

_____ **2.** We are brave.

_____ **3.** We like to go to school.

_____ **4.** We tell each other secrets.

_____ **5.** We like to help other people.

_____ **6.** We don't like it when we can't be together.

_____ **7.** We sometimes wish we could disappear.

_____ **8.** We like to eat the same foods.

Each of these sentences tells something about one of the characters in the stories you are going to read in this unit. As you read, you will find that you and your friend are a lot like the people in these stories.

1 Getting Ready to Read

Alarm clocks!

Just when you are really enjoying a dream, they go off!

What time do you get up on school days?

_____

1. What are three things you do in the morning to get ready for school?

☆ _____

☆ _____

☆ _____

2. When things go well, you're probably ready on time. But sometimes you may have to rush. Why? I wrote one reason for you. You write two more.

☆ _____

☆ *My brother won't get out of the bathroom.*

☆ _____

3. The girl in this story is named Alesia. In some ways Alesia is just like you. As you read this part of Alesia's story, what are two things you think you will find out?

☆ _____

☆ _____

Reading

Now read the story that begins on page 8. Answer the questions beside the story while you read.

Alesia

by Eloise Greenfield

Wed., March 19, 1980

This morning I woke up and looked at the clock. It said four-thirty. I said, "Uh-uh! This isn't me!" I rolled on over and went back to sleep. And then I overslept.

I get up at five-thirty on school days, because it takes me kind of a long time to do things. So this morning I had to rush to get dressed and eat and have all my books in the book bag by the time the school bus came at eight o'clock.

Daddy had put my wheelchair out front before he went to work, and the bus driver, Mr. Gordon, put it on the bus for me. Then Mrs. Smith, the bus attendant, came to my front door and I held on to her arm and walked to the bus.

What happened?

What can Alesia do now?

I can walk some now, if I hold on to a wall or a piece of furniture or somebody's arm, or if I push my wheelchair. I can even walk a little way without holding on to anything. And I remember when I couldn't do any of those things.

But I don't remember getting hit by that car. I only know what people tell me. My friend Valerie said she had been on the bike with me for a while, but I had let her off just before I started to race with Percy. I'm so glad she got off, so that she wasn't hurt, too. And I'm glad the doctors at the hospital didn't give up on me. They kept working on me and then they came out and said to Daddy and Mama, "We've done all we can. It's up to Alesia and the Lord now, it's up to her and the Lord."

I was unconscious for five weeks. A lot of people were praying for me, and some of them didn't even know me. Mama lit candles in the hospital chapel, and the priests at my church, St. Anthony's, said special prayers. And Sister Clotilde, she had been my teacher that year and I had been so bad in her class, always talking and stuff, but after I got hurt, she had her class praying for me twice a day.

What did other people do to help Alesia?

What does Alesia remember?

The day I woke up and started to talk, some of the nurses wanted me to surprise Mama. They wanted me to say, "Hi, Mama," when she walked into the room. But Daddy said no, he didn't know if she could stand the shock. So he called her at work and told her the good news. Mama says that after she got off the phone she just said four words—"My child is talking!" And she got out of there and came to the hospital as fast as she could.

I had my tenth birthday party in the hospital on October 8, 1972. I don't remember that, either, but the first time I went back to visit after I got out, something about that hospital just struck me. I said, "I remember this smell, yeah, I remember this smell!"

Thinking About What You Read

What did you find out?

1. Think of how you and Alesia are alike. What are three things Alesia says she has to do in the morning before getting on the school bus? List them here. Then put a check beside the things that you do in the morning, too.

MARCH 1980

Sunday	Monday	Tuesday	Wednesday	Thursday	Friday	Saturday
						1
2	3	4	5	6	7	8
9	10	11	12	13	14	15
16	17	18	19	20	21	22
23	24	25	26	27	28	29
30	31					

☆ _____

☆ _____

☆ _____

2. Now think of how you and Alesia are different. List at least two ways here.

☆ _____

☆ _____

How did the author help you read the story?

This part of Alesia's story is full of information about what happened to her. Ms. Greenfield really knows how to put a lot of facts together so you get important information fast. If you look back at the story, you will see that Ms. Greenfield uses two words to give you clues about the kinds of information she is going to write next.

1. One of the words the author uses is *And*. Ms. Greenfield starts some sentences with *And* to signal her readers that more information is coming up. And this information adds to what she just wrote.

Look back through the story. Find the sentences that start with *And*. Draw an arrow and a plus sign like this ➡ + under the word *And* to show that the next piece of information is added to the idea that came before it.

Did you find five sentences that use this pattern? Good.

2. The other signal word that Ms. Greenfield uses is *But*. Go back and find two sentences in the story that start with *But*. Underline the word *But* with an arrow like this ⟵ .

Ms. Greenfield uses the word *But* to signal her readers that the next piece

of information is _____ the idea she just wrote.
(Did you write "different from"?)

3. See if you can find two more places where Ms. Greenfield uses *and* and *but* to tell you more information. Look in the seventh paragraph and in the last paragraph. Mark these words like you did the others.

How can you use And *and* But *to signal readers about what you are going to write next?*

More than anything else about her hospital stay, Alesia remembers the smells. Make a list of smells that you remember. Tell what each smell makes you think about. I started the list for you.

SMELLS I REMEMBER	WHAT I THINK ABOUT
chlorine	*swimming at Red Bridge Pool with Beverly and Bobby*

Now choose one of your remembered smells to write a diary entry about. Use the space on page 14. As you write, use *and* when you want to add information to something you just said. Use *but* to give different information. When you are done, share your writing with a friend.

2 Getting Ready to Read

Don't look now... but there's someone—or something—watching you from inside this house.

Could it be... a ghost? NO! NO! NO! Not that! I'm scared of ghosts!

1. When you think of haunted houses, what kinds of things do you think of? Write some words that tell about haunted houses in the spaces below. I started the list for you.

dust balls   *dark halls*

HAUNTED HOUSES

2. What would make you go into a haunted house alone?

_____

_____

3. The story you are going to read is about a boy named Jimmy. He HAS to go into a haunted house to prove it isn't haunted. Jimmy's aunt is the owner of the house, so getting the key is not a problem. But when Jimmy gets to the house and goes up the front walk to the porch steps, his feet no longer want to take him any farther.

What do you think will happen to Jimmy when he finally gets up to the door and pushes it open?

_____

_____

Reading

See if you're right! Read this part of Jimmy's story, if you dare! It begins on page 16. Answer the questions beside the story as you read.

Jimmy Takes Vanishing Lessons

by
Walter R. Brooks

That was probably the bravest thing that Jimmy had ever done. He was in a long, dark hall with closed doors on both sides, and on the right, the stairs went up. He had left the door open behind him, and the light from it showed him that, except for the hatrack and table and chairs, the hall was empty. And then, as he stood there, listening to the bumping of his heart, gradually the light faded; the hall grew darker and darker—as if something huge had come up on the porch behind him and stood there, blocking the doorway. He swung round quickly, but there was nothing there. Nothing at all.

What did Jimmy see?

What happened?

Then what did Jimmy see?

He drew a deep breath. It must have been just a cloud passing across the sun. But then the door, all of itself, began to swing shut. And before he could stop it, it closed with a bang. And it was then, as he was pulling frantically at the handle to get out, that Jimmy saw the ghost.

It behaved just as you would expect a ghost to behave. It was a tall, dim, white figure, and it came gliding slowly down the stairs towards him. Jimmy gave a yell, yanked the door open, and tore down the steps.

He didn't stop until he was well down the road. Then he had to get his breath. He sat down on a log. "Boy!" he said. "I've seen a ghost! Golly, was that awful!" Then after a minute, he thought, "What was so awful about it? He was trying to scare me, like that smart aleck who is always jumping out from behind things. Pretty silly business for a grown-up ghost to be doing."

It always makes you mad when someone deliberately tries to scare you. And as soon as Jimmy got over his fright, he began to get angry. And he got up and started back. "I must get that key, anyway," he thought, for he had left it in the door.

Where did Jimmy go?

What did Jimmy do?

18

What was the ghost doing?

What happened to the ghost?

This time, he approached very quietly. He thought he'd just lock the door and go home. But, as he tiptoed up the steps, he saw it was still open, and as he reached cautiously for the key, he heard a faint sound. He drew back and peeked around the doorjamb, and there was the ghost.

The ghost was going back upstairs, but he wasn't gliding now, he was doing a sort of dance, and every other step he would bend double and shake with laughter. His thin cackle was the sound Jimmy had heard. Evidently, he was enjoying the joke he had played. That made Jimmy madder than ever. He stuck his head farther around the doorjamb and yelled "Boo!" at the top of his lungs. The ghost gave a thin shriek and leaped two feet in the air, then collapsed on the stairs.

Thinking About What You Read

What did you find out?

1. In what order did Jimmy do these things? Write the numbers **1–4** to show the order.

_____ He sat on a log.   _____ He tore down the steps.

_____ He gave a yell.   _____ He yanked the door open.

2. What made Jimmy do these things?

_____

_____

_____

3. What has someone done to try to scare you? What happened? Were you scared?

_____

_____

_____

4. What would you have done had you been Jimmy? Would you have gone back to the house to get the key? Why or why not?

_____

_____

_____

How did the author help you read the story?

Jimmy's story is full of action. To make it happen quickly, Mr. Brooks uses a lot of special words, called **verbs,** or **action words,** to tell what Jimmy did. The author made sure his verbs were used in **strong and colorful phrases.**

1. Read this sentence from the first paragraph of the story.

He swung round quickly, but there was nothing there.

Underline the verb phrase *swung round quickly.* These three words tell what Jimmy did and how he did it. Why do you think Mr. Brooks used these words instead of *turned really fast* or *looked behind him?*

_____

_____

2. Reread the story. Draw a box around other strong, colorful verbs and verb phrases that Mr. Brooks used to make the story interesting and exciting. Write three of your favorites here and tell why you like them.

_____

_____

_____

How can you use strong, colorful verbs and verb phrases to make a story interesting and exciting?

When did you do something brave that took all your courage? Tell about what you did and how you got the courage to do it. When you are finished, have a friend read your story. Ask your friend to circle your verb phrases and tell you how they made your writing exciting.

Getting Ready to Read

1. Look at the pictures around this page. What do these things make you think about?

   _____

   _____

   _____

2. What are three things that usually happen at Halloween parties? List them here.

   ☆ _____

   ☆ _____

   ☆ _____

3. I'll bet you wrote "Give a prize for the best costume" for one of the things, didn't you? If you were the person who had to choose the "best" costume, how would you make your decision? What kinds of things would make you think a costume is the "best"?

   _____

   _____

   _____

4. Now, imagine it's the day after the Halloween party. Imagine that *you* won the prize for the "best" costume. What will you say to your friends in school to tell them how you looked?

   _____

   _____

Reading

In the poem you are about to read, two characters are talking about how they think they look. I wonder if either of them will say the same things that you just wrote. Read the poem and find out.

Aunt Sponge and Aunt Spiker

by Roald Dahl

"I look and smell," Aunt Sponge declared,
  "as lovely as a rose!
Just feast your eyes upon my face,
  observe my shapely nose!
Behold my heavenly silky locks!
And if I take off both my socks
You'll see my dainty toes."
"But don't forget," Aunt Spiker cried,
  "how much your tummy shows!"

Aunt Sponge went red. Aunt Spiker said,
   "My sweet, you cannot win,
Behold MY gorgeous curvy shape,
   my teeth, my charming grin!
Oh, beauteous me! How I adore
My radiant looks! And please ignore
The pimple on my chin."
"My dear old trout!" Aunt Sponge cried out.
   "You're only bones and skin!"

Such loveliness as I possess can only truly shine
In Hollywood!" Aunt Sponge declared.
   "Oh, wouldn't that be fine!
I'd capture all the nations' hearts!
They'd give me all the leading parts!
The stars would all resign!"
"I think you'd make," Aunt Spiker said,
   "a lovely Frankenstein."

Thinking About What You Read

What did you find out?

1. One of the characters was fat, and the other one was thin. Which was which, and how did you figure that out?

_____

_____

_____

2. Look back at the words Aunt Sponge and Aunt Spiker used to describe how they looked. Would you use any of them to tell why your costume was picked "best" at the Halloween party? Which ones? List them here.

_____

_____

_____

How did the author help you read the poem?

Roald Dahl's poem is lots of fun! How come?

1. One of the reasons "Aunt Sponge and Aunt Spiker" is so much fun is because Mr. Dahl uses **exaggeration** to tell us about the characters. Reread the poem and draw a red line under the words Mr. Dahl uses to tell us how Aunt Sponge describes her smell. Now, use the red color to underline all the other words Mr. Dahl uses to describe Aunt Sponge. Draw a blue line under the words he uses to tell about Aunt Spiker.

2. Another reason the poem is fun to read is because Mr. Dahl uses **rhyme** to make the poem sound right. Reread the poem. Where are the rhyming words? Did you find two sets of words that rhyme in the first verse? Put boxes around the four words that rhyme with the same sound and circles around the two other words that rhyme. Now, see if you can find this same pattern in the other two verses.

3. Read the poem one more time. This time, tap your fingers together as you read the lines. Find the places in each line where you feel your fingers *have* to go together. This is where the beat or **rhythm** of the poem is. If we wrote the poem to show where the rhythm is, it could look like this:

"I **look** and **smell**," Aunt **Sponge** de**clared**," as **lovely as** a **rose**!"

How can you use exaggeration, rhyme, and rhythm to write your own poem?

1. Read this unfinished poem. Write some words in the blank spaces to finish it. Use exaggeration, rhyming words, and rhythm to help you do it.

Four Witches

Four witches rode the midnight sky.

As I looked up, they swept on by.

One witch's nose _____.

One witch's _____.

One witch's _____.

And the last witch's _____.

These witches were an ugly sight!

_____!

2. Show your finished poem to a friend. Ask your friend to put boxes around the rhyming words you used. See if your friend can tell where the beats of your poem are.

3. Compare your poem with the one your friend wrote. How did you both use exaggeration in your poems? Which of you used the best exaggeration? How can you tell?

_____

_____

_____

4 Getting Ready to Read

Have you ever thought about running away from home? I know I did. And so did lots of other kids just like me.

1. What are three reasons that someone might want to run away from home? Write your ideas here. I did one for you.

☆ _____

☆ _____

☆ *There are too many people in the family.*

2. Have you ever had to go stay with a relative or someone else you really didn't want to visit? How did you feel when you got there?

_____

_____

_____

3. In this part of the story of *Shoeshine Girl*, Sarah Ida thinks about running away and about having to stay with her aunt. What questions do you have about Sarah Ida before you read the selection?

_____

_____

_____

_____

Reading

Now read the story that begins on page 28. This part of the story is about the day Sarah Ida arrives in Palmville. See if you ever felt the way she does. Answer the questions beside the story as you read.

SHOE SHINE GIRL

by Clyde Robert Bulla

The train stopped at Palmville, and Sarah Ida had a sudden thought. What if she didn't get off? What if she just rode on to the end of the line? Maybe she could find a place where everything was new and she could start all over again.

But people would ask questions. *How old are you?... Only ten and a half? What are you doing here all by yourself?* Someone would be sure to find her and bring her back.

Who was waiting for Sarah Ida?

Anyway, it was too late. Aunt Claudia had already seen her. Aunt Claudia was at the station, looking through the train window and waving her thin hand.

Sarah Ida picked up her suitcase.

"Here, little lady, I'll help you with that," said the porter.

"I can carry it myself," she said, and she dragged it off the train.

Where is Sarah Ida from?

What kind of house does Aunt Claudia have?

Aunt Claudia gave her a kiss that smelled like cough drops. Then they took a taxi. They rode through town, and Aunt Claudia talked. "You've grown, but I knew you the minute I saw you. You've got your mother's pretty brown eyes, but you've got your father's jaw. Look—over there. That's our new supermarket. Things may seem quiet to you here, after the city, but I think you'll like Palmville. It's getting to be quite a city, too."

Sarah Ida said nothing.

"We're on Grand Avenue," said Aunt Claudia. "It's the main street." The taxi turned off the avenue and stopped in front of a square, gray house.

While Aunt Claudia paid the driver, Sarah Ida looked at the house. It was old, with a new coat of paint. It had spidery-looking porches and balconies.

They went inside.

Thinking About What You Read

What did you find out?

1. Sarah Ida had some questions about running away. Have you ever thought about questions like hers? Which ones?

_____

_____

_____

_____

2. Tell how you think Sarah Ida felt as she rode in the taxi with Aunt Claudia.

_____

_____

What did Sarah Ida do that made you think this was how she felt?

_____

_____

3. What words are used to tell about Aunt Claudia's house? Underline them in the story and draw a picture here of how her house might look.

How did the author help you read the story?

When Mr. Bulla starts this story, he wants his readers to know what Sarah Ida is thinking. To show a person's thoughts, he uses a special way of printing the words.

Reread the beginning of the story. Look at the second paragraph. Find the sentences that tell you what Sarah Ida thought. Draw one box around all these sentences.

Now look at the part of the second paragraph that you put the box around. You can see how Mr. Bulla used *italics* and a row of periods to help his readers know what Sarah Ida was thinking.

Italics make the words look different, so readers know they are important. When authors write by hand, they use <u>underlining</u> to show which words should be printed in *italics*. The row of three periods makes the reader slow down a little, so the words can be read just like the character would think them.

How can you use italics and a row of three periods to tell readers about what someone is thinking?

Here again are the words that Aunt Claudia spoke. Write the ideas, feelings, and questions Sarah Ida might be thinking as she listens to Aunt Claudia. <u>Draw a line under the words</u> you write that you want to be in *italics*. Try to use a row of three periods (...) to show where readers need to slow down as they read your ideas.

Aunt Claudia:

"You've grown, but I knew you the minute I saw you.

You've got your mother's pretty brown eyes, but you've got your father's jaw.

Sarah Ida:

_____

_____

_____

_____

_____

_____

_____

_____

_____

_____

Aunt Claudia: **Sarah Ida:**

Look—over there.
That's our new supermarket.

_____

_____

_____

Things may seem quiet to you
here, after the city, but I think
you'll like Palmville.

_____

_____

_____

_____

_____

It's getting to be quite a city,
too.

_____

_____

_____

_____

We're on Grand Avenue. It's
the main street."

_____

_____

_____

_____

Have a friend read Aunt Claudia's words as you read Sarah Ida's thoughts aloud.

Now, what do you think? Are you and Sarah Ida alike? List some ways that Sarah Ida is a kid just like you.

_____

_____

_____

_____

Getting Ready to Read

This story is from Japan. It is about an old man and an old woman.

1. What are two ways this story might begin?

☆ _____

☆ _____

2. The story goes on to say that one day the old man went to the mountains. The old woman went to the river. Why might each person have gone to these places?

Old Man—Mountains   Old Woman—River

_____   _____

_____   _____

While the old woman was at the river, she found a big peach floating in the water. She took it home as a gift for the old man. Later, as the old man was about to cut the big peach in half, a boy's voice came from inside the peach. Next, the peach opened and out jumped the boy. The old man and old woman called him Momotaro—Boy-of-the-Peach.

3. How might Momotaro be like you?

_____

_____

4. What are two questions you now have about this story?

☆ _____

☆ _____

Reading

Now read the story that begins on page 35. Answer the questions beside the story while you read.

MOMOTARO
Boy-of-the-Peach

by
Yoshiko Uchida

What does Momotaro ask to do?

One day Momotaro came before the old man and said, "You have both been good and kind to me. I am very grateful for all you have done, and now I think I am old enough to do some good for others too. I have come to ask if I may leave you."

"You wish to leave us, my son? But why?" asked the old man in surprise.

"Oh, I shall be back in a very short time," said Momotaro. "I wish only to go to the Island of the Ogres, to rid the land of those harmful creatures. They have killed many good people, and have stolen and robbed throughout the country. I wish to kill the ogres so they can never harm our people again."

"That is a fine idea, my son, and I will not stop you from going, " said the old man.

So that very day, Momotaro got ready to start out on his journey. The old woman prepared some millet cakes for him to take along on his trip, and soon Momotaro was ready to leave. The old man and woman were sad to see him go and called, "Be careful, Momotaro! Come back safely to us."

Why does Momotaro want to leave?

What did the old woman make for him?

"Yes, yes, I shall be back soon," he answered. "Take care of yourselves while I am away," he added, and waved as he started down the path toward the forest.

He hurried along, for he was anxious to get to the Island of the Ogres. While he was walking through the cool forest where the grass grew long and high, he began to feel hungry. He sat down at the foot of a tall pine tree and carefully unwrapped the *furoshiki* which held his little millet cakes. "My, they smell good," he thought. Suddenly, he heard the tall grass rustle and saw something stalking through the grass toward him. Momotaro blinked hard when he saw what it was. It was a dog as big as a calf! But Momotaro was not frightened, for the dog just said,"Momotaro-san, Momotaro-san, what is it you are eating that smells so good?"

What did he see?

"I'm eating a delicious millet cake which my good mother made for me this morning," he answered.

The dog licked his chops and looked at the cake with hungry eyes. "Please, Momotaro-san," he said, "just give me one of your millet cakes, and I will come along with you to the Island of the Ogres. I know why you are going there, and I can be of help to you."

"Very well, my friend," said Momotaro. "I will take you along with me," and he gave the dog one of his millet cakes to eat.

What did Momotaro decide to do?

Thinking About What You Read

What did you find out?

1. Think of three words that tell what kind of person Momotaro is. Write them here.

_____

_____

2. Which of the words that tell about Momotaro also tell about you?

_____

_____

Why do these words tell about you?

_____

_____

_____

_____

3. Momotaro is going to the Island of the Ogres. What do you think this place will be like? Name at least one problem you think Momotaro might have there.

_____

_____

_____

_____

4. What are two ways a dog might be useful to Momotaro when he gets to the island?

☆ _____

_____

☆ _____

_____

5. What other animals might be useful to Momotaro on the Island of the Ogres? What could they help him do?

Animals	What They Could Do
_____	_____
_____	_____
_____	_____
_____	_____

How did the author help you read the story?

Like all storytellers, Yoshiko Uchida needs to use words that tell readers about the times when things happen in the story. To do this, she uses phrases like *Once upon a time, One day,* or *In a little while.*

1. Reread the story. Find and underline these **time words.**

One day   So that very day   and soon

　　　　　While   Suddenly

2. Now make a list of at least four more words or phrases you know that tell about time.

☆ _____

☆ _____

☆ _____

☆ _____

How can you use time words to tell readers when things in a story happened?

To tell more about Momotaro's story—and to show how a storyteller uses time words—we can use a circle pattern like the one on page 41. Read the events that are written around the circle.

Use the time words in the circle to make up the rest of Momotaro's story. Remember that Momotaro told the old man he would come home. Try to get Momotaro back home by the end of the story. When you are done, you might like to rewrite your ideas in the usual form of a story so that you can share it with friends.

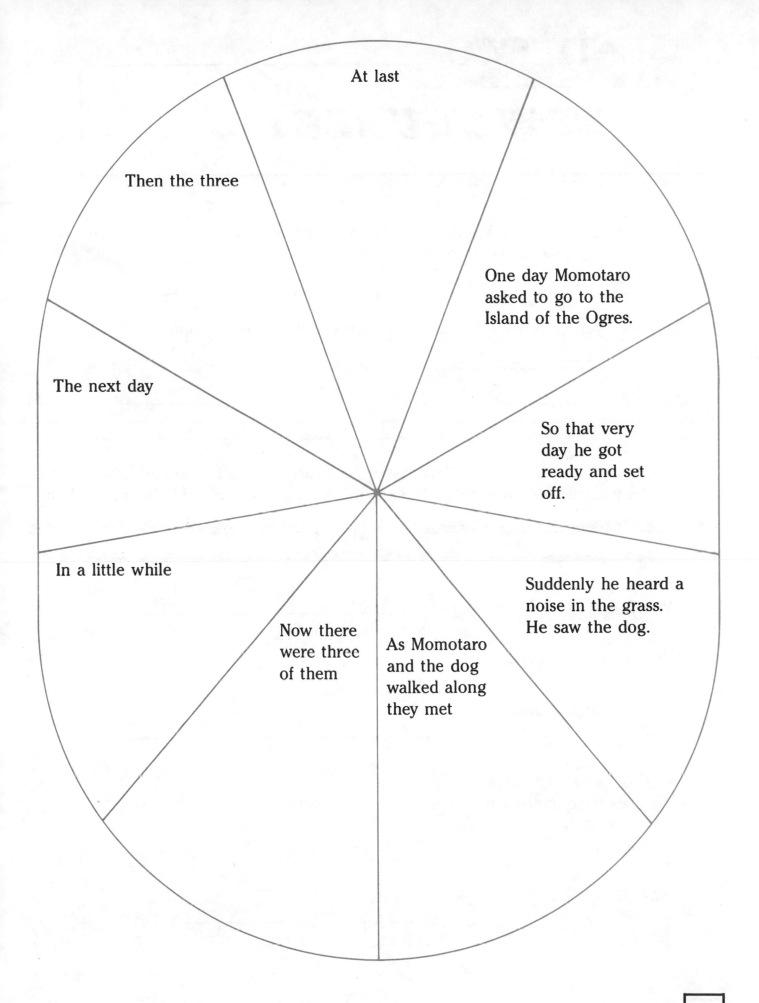

At last

Then the three

The next day

In a little while

Now there were three of them

As Momotaro and the dog walked along they met

One day Momotaro asked to go to the Island of the Ogres.

So that very day he got ready and set off.

Suddenly he heard a noise in the grass. He saw the dog.

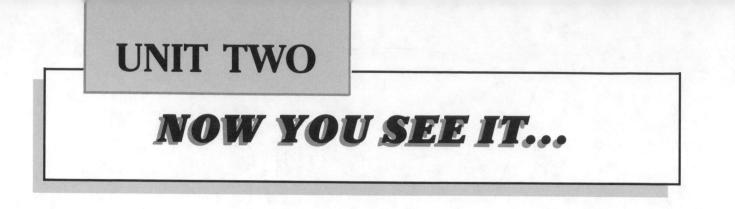

NOW YOU SEE IT...

1. Read the title of this unit. What words almost always come next when you hear, *"Now you see it,..."*? Write those words here.

_____

2. When have you used these words? What were you trying to tell someone?

_____

_____

_____

3. Now look at the following WANTED poster. Read each description and tell who or what might be wanted. Would you want to find "it"? If so, put a star beside the description.

WANTED

Was first seen in the fog. _____

Was wearing an overcoat. _____

Had chalkdust around its
mouth. _____

Left footprints that were
3 inches wide and seven
inches long. Each foot had
six toes. _____

Was also seen in your
school. _____

4. Remember that the title of this unit is *NOW YOU SEE IT...* How could each idea on the poster fit in the unit? Here's the WANTED poster again. This time, complete it by telling what might have happened to make each thing disappear.

WANTED

THINGS GONE	WHERE IT WENT
Seen in the fog.	_____
Wore an overcoat.	_____
Had chalkdust on its mouth.	_____
Left footprints.	_____
Was on the desk.	_____

I wonder, did you think about the same ideas as the authors of the five stories in this unit? Each one tells about *NOW YOU SEE IT, NOW YOU DON'T.* See how your ideas match those in the stories.

Getting Ready to Read

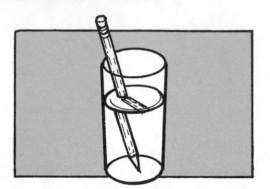

1. Look at the pencil in the glass of water. How many parts does it

appear to have? _____

2. How many parts does the pencil

really have? _____

Why does the pencil in the glass seem to be broken? Because your eyes and your brain fooled you, that's why!

3. When have you looked at something and thought you saw something else? Tell about what you thought you saw. Then tell what the thing really was.

_____

_____

_____

4. Look at the pictures in the story that you are about to read. Tell what these pictures make you think about.

_____

_____

5. What is one thing you expect to find out as you read this story?

_____

_____

Reading

Now read the story that begins on page 45. Answer the questions beside the story as you read. See if you find out what you thought you would.

Mirages: Nature's Tricks

by
Dotti Kauffman

What are two things your eyes do for you?

Of all your senses, sight may be one of the most important. Your eyes probably tell you more about the world than any of your other senses.

You use your eyes to do lots of everyday things. When you get dressed, your eyes help you find the right color clothes to wear together. When you borrow a marker from a friend, your eyes tell you how far away the marker is and where you have to reach for it.

Most of the time you believe what your eyes tell you. But you have probably noticed that sometimes your eyes can fool you.

Picture this. It is summertime. It's a hot day. The sun is beating down on the trees, the bushes, the car in which you are riding, and the road ahead. The temperature in the car is rising higher and higher. You are thirsty. You can only think of getting water. Thoughts of "Water! Where can I get some water?" run through your mind.

Then suddenly, just up ahead ... on the road ... is ... water! A pool of cool, rippling water lies just "up there."

But when you get "there," your eyes tell you the water is yet farther ahead. As you keep going down the road, you find the pool just can't be reached. It is a **mirage.** What your eyes and brain have told you is there is not real.

The water mirage is one of the most common **optical illusions** in nature. Optical illusions happen when your brain misunderstands what your eyes see. You think you see water on the road ahead because in the bright summer sun, the surface of the road gets very hot. It then heats the air just above it. As the heated air rises and moves, it bends any light rays passing through it. They seem to shimmer. That's what you "see" when you see that gleaming pond of water.

What is the water?

What does heated air do?

Here's another mirage you can see on a hot summer day. Look across the top of a car that has been sitting in the sun for a long time. Try to see a tree or another object that is some distance away. The object will seem to shimmer or sparkle because the air just above the top of the car roof is warmer than the air a little higher. But, if you walk around the car and look at the same object, it will no longer seem to shimmer. It will look the way you expect it to look.

Mirages are one of nature's best tricks.

What are mirages?

Thinking About What You Read

What did you find out?

1. What two things are needed to see a mirage?

☆ _____

☆ _____

2. When have you seen a water mirage like the one described in the story?

_____

_____

_____

3. How does being hot and thirsty make you believe the water mirage is really water—this time?

_____

_____

_____

4. What sounds might you hear when you reach the place where the water mirage is? Why?

_____

_____

_____

How did the author help you read the story?

When I wrote this story, I wanted you to "see" the water mirage in your mind. To help you do this, I told you to think about the sun on a hot summer day. You know the sun is up in the sky. I told you it was beating down on the trees, the bushes, the car, and the road. By telling you these things in this order, I was trying to lead you to think in the direction of top-down.

1. Reread the story and find the paragraph that has this top-down order of information and underline the exact sentence. Now, draw a picture here of what this sentence tells you.

2. Now look at the second-to-last paragraph of the story. Find and underline the sentences that tell you to "look" in a bottom-up order. Then draw a picture here of what these sentences describe.

How can you use top-down or bottom-up order to tell readers information?

1. Look around your classroom. Find a crack in the ceiling or a mark on a desk that looks like something else. Write a description of what you think you see, telling about it from the top-down or the bottom-up.

_____

_____

_____

_____

_____

_____

_____

_____

_____

_____

_____

_____

2. Ask a friend to read your description and draw a picture of what you described. Then have your friend find the place in the classroom that made you see what you wrote about.

3. Look at your place in the classroom again. This time, think of it as the crack or spot it really is. What happens to the object you thought you saw?

_____

_____

_____

_____

Getting Ready to Read

Fog! Fog everywhere!

Think about fog and when you have seen it. What is it? What color is it? How does the fog feel? How does it make *you* feel?

1. Think about your answers to these questions. Then fill in the circles in this diagram.

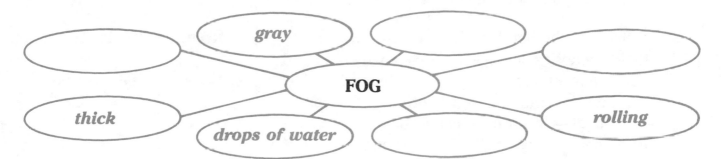

2. Have you ever been out in the fog? What do you remember about it? Who was with you? Why were you in the fog? What happened?

_____

_____

_____

_____

3. What are three things people might think they see in the fog?

_____

How would these three things look in the bright sunshine?

_____

Reading

Now read the story that begins on page 52. Answer the questions beside the story as you read.

Fog Magic

by Julia L. Sauer

It was just as they turned out of the path to the cove and into the Old Road that Greta happened to look off to the south.

"Rosie, wait," she called sharply.

She caught her breath and stared. If only stupid old Rosie could see it, too. Surely there was the outline of a building. It was blurred and indistinct, but those straight upright lines, that steep angle—no spruces could look *that* way. Greta's heart almost stopped beating, but she had no silly feeling of fear. Fog had always seemed to her like the magic spell in the old fairy tales—a spell that caught you up and kept you as safe, once you were inside it, as you would have been within a soap bubble. But this was stranger than anything she had ever seen before. Here was a house—a house where no house stood! Indistinct though it was, she could follow every line of it. A high sharp roof, a peaked gable, a little lean-to at the side. It was all there. Just such a house as those she saw every day in the village.

Rosie? Who is Rosie?

What did Greta see?

"So this," she said to herself, "*this* is what can happen to you in a fog. I always knew that there must be something hidden."

It was the most exciting thing that had ever happened to her in her whole life. Rosie, far ahead, was mooing at the pasture bars, and Greta tore herself away to follow. Once inside the barn, she wished that she had stayed and gone closer.

She stood in the barn doorway looking out across the yard. The fog was dense and gray. It blanketed the yard and made the house across the intervening feet as dim as that other one had been. Behind her in the quiet sweet-smelling barn her father was milking.

"Father," Greta spoke softly.

"Yes? What is it, Greta?" The milk streamed rhythmically into the pail.

Rosie? Who is Rosie?

Where did Greta go?

How does her own house look?

"Father, down where the path to Little Cove turns off the Old Road, is there—is there any old house off in the spruces to the south?"

Her father never stirred on the milking stool, but he dropped his hands quietly on his knees. The barn was very still for a moment.

"There's an old cellar hole off there, Greta," he said at last. "There's been no house upon it in my day." His voice was as calm and slow as ever. And then he added something very strange. "Every cellar hole should have a house," he said quietly.

"Yes, Father," Greta answered. It was almost as if he'd told her that *she* should build a house and she had almost promised.

What did Greta think her father meant?

Thinking About What You Read

What did you find out?

1. How had fog always seemed to Greta? Does it seem that way to you, too?

_____

_____

_____

_____

_____

2. Was the house Greta saw on the Old Road really there? Or did she just think it was? How do you know?

_____

_____

_____

_____

_____

3. What do you think the end of the story means? Put a check beside the sentence that best tells your ideas.

_____ Greta is to build a house using nails, wood, and bricks.

_____ Greta is to go explore the house in the fog the next time it appears.

_____ Greta should follow her feelings and do whatever she needs to do to build the house. This may mean she is to use fog magic.

How did the author help you read the story?

Ms. Sauer wants her readers to see the people, places, and things she is telling about in the story. To help her readers picture them easily and clearly, Ms. Sauer uses **synonyms.** These are words that mean the same, or almost the same, thing.

1. In the third sentence of the third paragraph, Ms. Sauer writes that Greta saw "the outline of a building." Now, you know outlines are sketches or drawings that are not complete. But Ms. Sauer wants to be certain that you really understand what Greta saw. So Ms. Sauer uses the words *blurred* and *indistinct* to tell more about the sight Greta was seeing. If we drew a diagram of how these words work together, it might look like this:

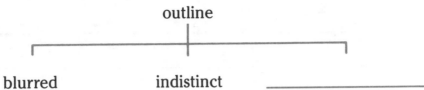

Did you notice the blank space in the diagram? Later in the story, Ms. Sauer uses another word to describe Greta's own house. This word means almost the same thing as *blurred* and *indistinct*. Find the word on page 54 and write it in the blank space.

2. Ms. Sauer uses *blurred, indistinct,* and *dim* to help you understand what she means. What are some other words that mean almost the same thing? Make a list of synonyms here. Use a thesaurus if you have one.

_____   _____   _____

_____   _____   _____

How can you use synonyms to make your writing clearer?

LOST IN THE FOG! Search through the fog to find the letters you need to finish the eight words below it. Then sort the words into two groups of synonyms, or words that mean almost the same thing.

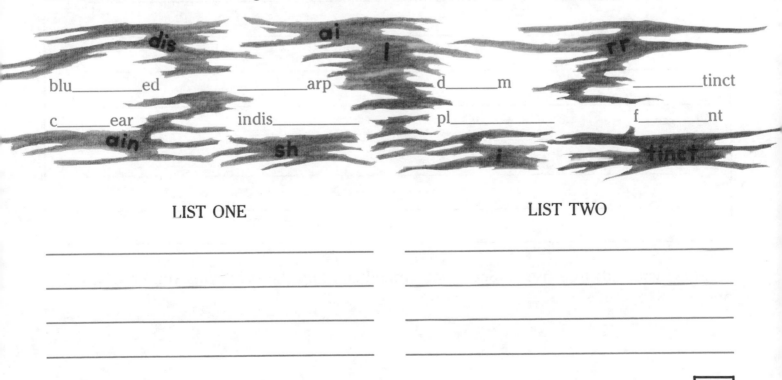

LIST ONE   LIST TWO

_____   _____

_____   _____

_____   _____

_____   _____

Use your two lists of words to write two travel ads. Write one ad to make people want to visit Greta's fog house. Write the other ad to tell about the same place as it might look on a bright sunny day.

AD ONE

_____

_____

_____

_____

_____

_____

_____

AD TWO

_____

_____

_____

_____

_____

_____

_____

Show your ads to a friend. See if your friend can find the synonyms you used in each one.

Getting Ready to Read

What's going on here?

Maps are gone! There's no chalk! Books are disappearing one by one! Pencils and homework papers, too!

Could the student in this picture be you? Have you ever wished that you'd never have to do schoolwork again? (It's okay. You can be honest. I won't tell.)

1. Suppose you *could* make things in your classroom disappear. How would you do it? Write two ideas here.

☆ _____

☆ _____

2. Suppose you could even make your teacher disappear. What time of the day would you choose to do it? Why?

_____

_____

Reading

As you might suspect, the poem you are going to read tells about events just like these. See if the poet's ideas are in any way like yours. Turn the page to begin reading.

Creature in the Classroom

by
Jack Prelutsky

It appeared inside our classroom
at a quarter after ten,
it gobbled up the blackboard,
three erasers and a pen.
It gobbled teacher's apple
and it bopped her with the core.
"How dare you!" she responded.
"You must leave us...there's the door."

The Creature didn't listen
but described an arabesque
as it gobbled all her pencils,
seven notebooks and her desk.
Teacher stated very calmly,
"Sir! You simply cannot stay,
I'll report you to the principal
unless you go away!"

But the thing continued eating,
it ate paper, swallowed ink,
as it gobbled up our homework
I believe I saw it wink.
Teacher finally lost her temper.
"Out!" she shouted at the creature.
The creature hopped beside her
and GLOPP...it swallowed teacher.

Thinking About What You Read

What did you find out?

1. Why do you think the creature arrived "at a quarter after ten"?

_____

_____

2. Do you think this creature knows any manners? Why or why not?

_____

_____

3. We humans group our food into classes like fruit, vegetables, dairy products, and grains. The creature in the poem also seems to like certain groups of food. List the foods the creature ate that fit into the groups below.

Tree Products	Fruits	Meats	Other
_____	_____	_____	_____
_____	_____	_____	_____
_____	_____	_____	_____
_____	_____	_____	_____

4. Why do you think I put this poem in a unit called **Now You See It...?**

_____

_____

How did the author help you read the poem?

1. Mr. Prelutsky probably had a good time when he wrote this poem. To help his readers enjoy his ideas, the poet wrote about things that are found in almost every school. Make a list of the things named in the poem that you have in your school.

_____

_____

2. Mr. Prelutsky also used exclamation marks (!) and CAPITAL LETTERS to show readers that he was feeling strongly about what happened. Reread the poem. Circle all the words and sentences that are followed by an exclamation mark. Underline the word that appears in all CAPITAL LETTERS.

What else did Mr. Prelutsky use to help you read the poem? Of course! You're right! He used rhyme and rhythm.

How can you use the names of familiar things, exclamation marks, and capital letters to tell readers what you are thinking?

Think about what happened in this poem. Who or what else in school would you like to make disappear? I started a list for you. You add a few more ideas.

halls _____ _____

glue _____ _____

door knobs _____ _____

Now write a fourth verse for the poem. Tell what the creature did next. Be sure to use exclamation points, capital letters, rhyme, and rhythm just the way Mr. Prelutsky did.

Still the thing continued eating,

it ate books, it sniffed _____

_____

_____

_____

_____

_____

_____

_____

_____

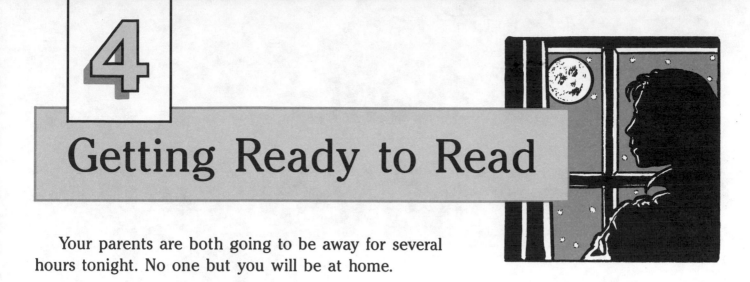

Getting Ready to Read

Your parents are both going to be away for several hours tonight. No one but you will be at home.

1. What can you do to make sure you are safe while you are alone? I started a list for you. Add three more things.

Things I'd Do to Keep Safe

☆ *Lock the doors.* _____

☆ _____

☆ _____

☆ _____

2. What are three things you might do to keep yourself busy while you are alone?

Things I'd Do to Keep Busy

☆ _____

☆ _____

☆ _____

3. Okay, you are alone. Suddenly you hear a loud SCREECH! It came from just outside the kitchen window! What could have made that awful sound? Add two of your own ideas to this list.

☆ *A Windigo, the monster that leaves footprints of flames, came out of the woods.*

☆ _____

☆ _____

Reading

Carefully, now! Read the story that begins on page 64. Answer the questions beside the story as you read.

The Night the Monster Came Out

by
Mary Calhoun

One night Andy was alone in the house. His father was working the night shift for the Sheriff's Department, and his mother had to go to real-estate classes that week at the Community Center, a mile away.

"The Trents are home next door," Mom said.

Each house, however, sat on its own half-acre of land, so "next door" wasn't exactly on the other side of the driveway.

How quickly can
Andy's mom be home?

"I can be home in three minutes, if you have any trouble," Mom said. "You sure you won't be afraid?"

"Aw, Mom, no!"

Andy grinned and hoped his freckles were staying put. Mom said his freckles stood out when he was scared.

She'd only be going to class three nights, he reminded himself. It was important. Mom was excited about learning to sell real estate.

What happened to the
garage door?

After Mom backed the car out, she remembered to work the door-closing device. It rolled the garage door down and locked it automatically. Good old Mom.

Andy checked around. All the doors were locked. All the curtains were drawn against the black night. The telephone worked. He didn't turn on the television, because there might be a scary show. Mom said he watched too much TV, anyway.

Andy settled down to read for his book report. *Stock-Car Racing* was a good safe book to be reading when you're alone in the house.

The house was awfully quiet. Maybe he ought to turn on the television real loud. No, for if there were any strange sounds, he wouldn't hear them.

Andy read on, turned a page.

Screech. Andy's heart jumped. A shriek came faintly from outside! The Windigo!

No, he told himself right away. It was an owl. He'd heard that kind of screech before, and it was always an owl.

Just the same, Andy knelt on the couch and peered out between the drapes. It was snowing. A spring snowstorm had set in. Gently snow was beginning to speckle the ground. He couldn't see an owl. Or anything else unusual. The yellow porch light shone softly on the snow.

What did Andy do?

What did Andy hear?

What did Andy hear this time?

Now, think about something: what will happen to these footprints in a little while?

Andy kept on reading, and his heart quit going so fast. He finished the chapter. Another chapter.

And the garbage can clanged.

It's the neighbor dogs, Andy told himself. The neighbor dogs were after the garbage again.

He went out to the kitchen. Carefully he pinched aside a curtain and peered out at the garbage can. There was a thin layer of snow on the ground.

And in the snow...around the garbage can...were *giant footprints*.

Thinking About What You Read

What did you find out?

1. Look back at page 63. What things did you say you would do to keep safe if you were home alone? What things did Andy do that are the same?

_____

_____

_____

2. Why was *Stock-Car Racing* a good book for Andy to read?

_____

_____

3. Who or what do you think made the footprints? Why?

_____

_____

_____

How did the author help you read the story?

1. In the very first sentence of this story, you read that Andy is alone in the house. In the very next sentence, Ms. Calhoun tells you **why.** She wastes no time in telling you the **cause** of the situation. Look at this cause-and-effect chart. I've given you one reason why Andy is by himself. You fill in the other reason.

CAWSE ► ► ► ► ► ► ► ► ►	EFFECT
Andy's father worked the night shift. _____	► ► Andy was home alone.

2. Ms. Calhoun tells her readers more causes and effects as she continues with the story of Andy's night alone. Go back to the story and find the information you need to finish the cause-and-effect chart at the top of the next page.

CAUSE ▶ ▶ ▶ ▶ ▶ ▶ ▶ ▶ ▶		EFFECT
	▶	▶ Andy's freckles stood out.
Mom used the door-closing device. ▶	▶	
	▶	▶ Andy did not turn on TV.
Andy heard a screech. ▶	▶	
	▶	▶ Andy looked out between the drapes.
The garbage can clanged. ▶	▶	

How can you use cause-and-effect information in your writing?

In this part of the story, you read about what Andy did <u>inside</u> the house. What was going on <u>outside</u> the house? What really caused the garbage can to clang? What really made the giant footprints? Use the space below to tell what was going on. Remember to explain the causes and effects of the events that happen in your story.

5 Getting Ready to Read

GRAND AM

A great car.
Low mileage.
Silver.

E250

CD player,
sunroof,
new tires,
one owner.

SPITFIRE

Runs great!
Body rusted.
Needs tune-up.
Cheap!

BEETLE CLASSIC

New brakes,
carpet, paint.
Must see!

Your big brother just asked you to help him choose which used car to buy. Look at the ads on this page. Which car would you want your brother to buy? Draw a circle around the ad for it.

1. Why did you choose the ad that you circled?

_____

_____

2. What kinds of things can go wrong with a used car? Make a list of four things here.

☆ _____

☆ _____

☆ _____

☆ _____

3. Now, look at page 71 and read just the title of this story. What does the title make you think the story might be about? I started a list of possible ideas. You add two more.

☆ *One day a gangster gets in the back seat and makes the driver help rob a bank.*

☆ _____

☆ _____

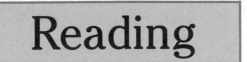

Reading

Now read the story and see if any of your ideas are in it. Answer the questions beside the story as you read.

The Gangster in the Back Seat

by Maria Leach

What did they see?

Once a young couple, out shopping for an old used car, wandered into a used-car lot and began to look over what was there. Suddenly they came upon a late-model Packard standing among the old wrecks.

It shone. It gleamed. It looked perfect.

They asked the price, never for a minute expecting to be able to buy it. The price was ridiculously low. The car seemed absolutely perfect. All right. They would buy it.

"You don't want that car," said the manager of the lot.

Oh, but they did!

"Everybody buys it brings it back!" he said.

What did the manager tell them?

But they bought it. They could not imagine ever giving it up.

And they were just as delighted after the car was theirs. They took long blissful rides together. They could hardly believe their luck.

But the first time either of them went out alone (usually the young wife) it was another story.

The first time the young woman drove the car by herself, she kept feeling as if someone were in the back seat. She would turn her head and look, and of course no one was there. But the feeling persisted.

What did the woman see?

One day as she glanced in the rear-view mirror she saw two ugly, leering eyes looking right into hers.

She stopped the car and turned to look. But there was no one there.

Sometimes she would smell the heavy smell of a strong cigar. But when she looked, there was no one there.

What did the man see?

What did the couple do with the car?

The young woman said nothing of all this to her husband. He too would see the face in the mirror or smell the cigar. But they never said a word to each other.

Time went by and the lone driver began to hear the voice of this back-seat ghost: an ugly voice, ugly words—never a full sentence.

The day finally came when neither one could stand it any longer. They confessed their experiences to each other and they took the car back.

"You saw him, too, huh?" said the used-car dealer. "Couldn't stand that cigar, huh?"

"Who *is* he?" the young couple asked.

And the story ends with the terrifying gangster in the back seat being some well-known hood of the Al Capone empire, who had been taken for the proverbial ride and rubbed out in his own car—that very car. And so the car turned up in the used-car lot—again and again and again. Every buyer was terrified of the terrifying face in the rear-view mirror and terrified of the terrifying voice.

Everyone who bought it brought it back.

Thinking About What You Read

What did you find out?

1. What were two reasons the young couple bought this car?

_____

_____

2. Did this story happen last year? How do you know?

_____

_____

3. What things happened to let the wife and husband know that the gangster was in the back seat? List them in order here.

_____

_____

How did the author help you read the story?

Ms. Leach tells this story of the gangster quickly. She tells us who and what without giving us a lot of facts. Her story does not even include the names of the characters. We really don't need to know their names because what happened to them is more important than who they are.

To help her tell the story quickly, Ms. Leach uses words like *they, she,* and *he* to let readers know who is doing something. These words are called **pronouns.** They are words that can be used to take the place of nouns.

1. Reread the story and match the pronouns with the nouns they replace. Use a yellow crayon to draw a circle around the word *couple.* Then look a little further in the story and find a pronoun that stands for *couple.* Underline this word in yellow every time it appears in the story and means "the couple."

2. Use a blue crayon to draw a circle around the nouns that name the car. Then underline in blue all the pronouns in the story that mean "the car."

3. Use a black crayon to mark the nouns and pronouns that mean "the gangster" throughout the story.

How can you use pronouns to tell a story quickly?

Ghost stories are often of the **"Now You See It..."** kind. Think of a ghost story you have heard and tell it in a short, fast way. Try to use only the nouns you must and then use pronouns to make the story move quickly. Write your story here.

If you can, share your story with some friends. Try telling it in a dark room!

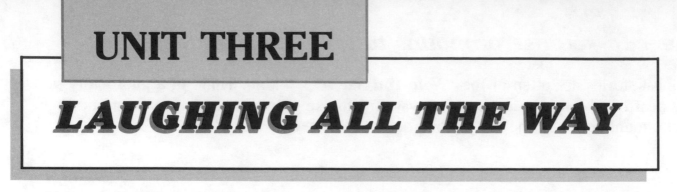

UNIT THREE

LAUGHING ALL THE WAY

Have you laughed today?

Say, that could be a good saying for a bumper sticker! Laughter makes people feel good. Laughter helps people forget their problems, if only for a little while.

1. What other sayings about laughter or laughing might be good daily reminders for people to laugh? Finish this idea and then write a saying of your own.

A laugh a day _____.

_____

_____

2. What things make people laugh? Name some in the circles below. I started the ideas for you. If you need to, add more circles.

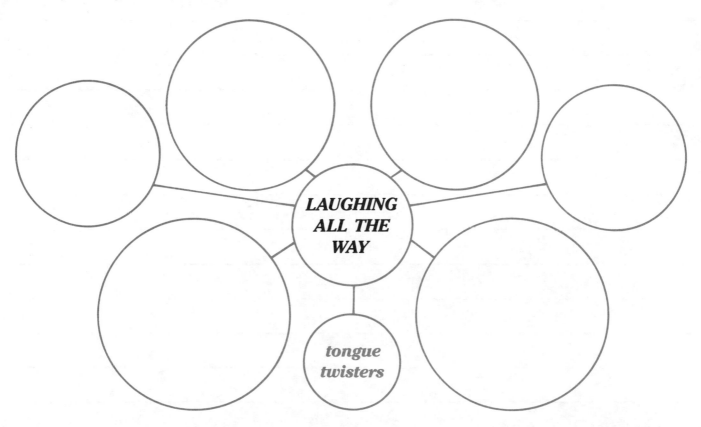

Each of the stories in this unit has something funny in it. As you read them, you may find yourself LAUGHING ALL THE WAY!

Getting Ready to Read

Often, people are honored by being awarded banners. Read the banners below. Who might get each one? Name the person you would choose and write the person's name on that banner.

WORLD'S BEST PIZZA MAKER	**WORLD'S BEST SINGER**
_____	_____
WORLD'S FUNNIEST MAN	**WORLD'S FUNNIEST WOMAN**
_____	_____

The story you are going to read is about Bill Cosby. Draw a banner to give him. Then tell why you chose the banner you did.

_____

_____

All these banners tell only one thing about the person they were made for. What are some other things you would like to know about Bill Cosby? List your questions here.

_____

_____

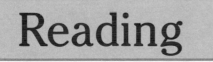

Reading

Now read the story that begins on page 78. Answer the questions beside the story as you read. Look for the answers to your own questions, too.

BILL COSBY

by George Zanderbergen

The joke's on him.

Bill Cosby comes out to do his comedy act. And the people start smiling before he ever says a word. They know he is going to tell stories about himself. Stories about growing up in the city.

Maybe he'll tell about how he and his brother used their bed for a trampoline until their father caught them. Or about the time he listened to a spooky radio program about the chicken heart that ate New York.

He may tell about his friend, Old Weird Harold, who was 6-foot-9 and weighed 50 pounds. And how one night they were coming home late over the 9th Street Bridge and this monster came out of a dark alley.

Or the time Fat Albert won the buck-buck championship by squashing the kids from the other neighborhood. Or the time that Junior Barnes hit Bill with a slushball, so Bill decided to get revenge and put a snowball into the freezer until July.

You'd better believe it, man! Hey-hey-hey! That's Bill Cosby.

What will Bill tell?

What kind of man is Bill?

What do Bill's stories help him do?

Bill Cosby is a very funny man. When you listen to the comical stories about his childhood, you might think that his early life was one long joke. But you would be wrong.

"I am two people," Bill Cosby has said. "One is the cat up there entertaining and enjoying every minute of it. I like to stand up and give. Let it all hang out! Then there's this other cat. His father drank. His mother transferred her love to her three sons. They started out in the middle class when dad was young and working. Dropped to lower class and then the projects. Get the picture?"

Bill talks mostly about his funny memories. But the other kind are there, too. His clowning has been a way to forget the sad things. By laughing he made it easier to put up with fear, with loneliness, with poverty.

Thinking About What You Read

What did you find out?

1. What story does Bill Cosby tell that is about something you have done too?

_____

_____

2. What makes Old Weird Harold weird?

_____

_____

3. Do you think there really was a kid exactly like Old Weird Harold? Why or why not?

_____

_____

4. Is Bill Cosby like someone you know? How?

_____

_____

_____

How did the author help you read the story?

Writers have many ways of making their writing funny and interesting. To do this, they must **plan** what to include in their stories, what to leave out, and what order to put things in.

1. What are some things Mr. Zanderbergen probably did before he wrote this story? Make a list here. I started it for you.

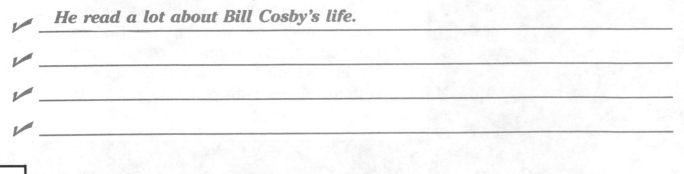

      He read a lot about Bill Cosby's life. _____

      _____

      _____

      _____

2. After Mr. Zanderbergen did these things, he had to plan *how* he was going to tell Mr. Cosby's life story. One way authors can plan what they will write is to make an **outline** of their ideas first. Mr. Zanderbergen's story follows an outline. Let's find it together.

You know that outlines show main ideas and details. You also know that outlines use roman numerals to mark the main ideas and capital letters to mark details.

Read the sentences in the outline below. Then look back at the story and find the place where each item is written. In the story itself, underline the main idea with a red crayon and the details with a blue crayon.

I. Bill Cosby tells stories about himself.

A. Bill and his brother used their bed for a trampoline.

B. Bill listened to a spooky radio program about the chicken heart that ate New York.

C. Bill may tell stories about _____

_____

D. Bill may tell about the time _____

_____

E. Or Bill may tell about the time he put a snowball _____

_____

Now go back and complete the outline above. Use the sentences you underlined in the story to help you finish it.

How can you use an outline to plan what you will write?

When Mr. Zanderbergen planned this story, he used an outline. When Bill Cosby plans a comedy act, he uses an outline. Suppose that you are going to plan your own comedy act. You too need to use an outline. Here's one way to do it.

First, think about some jokes you can remember. How many do you know about animals? How many do you know about people? How many others do you know, and what are they about?

Next make a list of the jokes you want to tell and write a brief note about them under each of the main ideas. Use the outline form on the next page.

I. I know jokes about animals.

A. _____

_____

B. _____

_____

C. _____

_____

II. I know jokes about people.

A. _____

_____

B. _____

_____

C. _____

_____

III. I know jokes about _____.

A. _____

_____

B. _____

_____

C. _____

_____

Look back over your outline. Think about your jokes. Try telling them to yourself in this order. Then try telling them to a friend. Why does making the outline help you to remember your jokes and to tell them well?

_____

_____

_____

Getting Ready to Read

You probably know the story of *Charlotte's Web.* It's about a spider named Charlotte and a pig named Wilbur.

1. Even if you don't know the story, can you think of two reasons why a spider and a pig might be friends? Write them here.

☆ _____

☆ _____

2. What other animals might also be friends with Charlotte and Wilbur?

_____

_____

3. Suppose all these friends got together to talk about a problem. What sounds might you hear, if you were nearby?

_____

_____

4. What would be funny about a group of animals having a meeting?

_____

_____

Reading

You need to know that several days ago Charlotte wrote "Some Pig!" in one of her webs. Read the part of the story that begins on page 84 to find out why she did this and what the problem is. Answer the questions beside the story while you read.

Charlotte's Web

by E. B. White

One evening, a few days after the writing had appeared in Charlotte's web, the spider called a meeting of all the animals in the barn cellar.

"I shall begin by calling the roll. Wilbur?"

"Here!" said the pig.

"Gander?"

"Here, here, here!" said the gander.

"You sound like three ganders," muttered Charlotte. "Why can't you just say 'here'? Why do you have to repeat everything?"

"It's my idio–idio–idiosyncrasy," replied the gander.

Who was in charge?

"Goose?" said Charlotte.

"Here, here, here," said the goose. Charlotte glared at her.

"Goslings, one through seven?"

"Bee–bee–bee!" "Bee–bee–bee!" "Bee–bee–bee!" "Bee–bee–bee!" "Bee–bee–bee!" "Bee–bee–bee!" "Bee–bee–bee!" said the goslings.

"This is getting to be quite a meeting," said Charlotte. "Anybody would think we had three ganders, three geese, and twenty-one goslings. Sheep?"

"He–aa–aa!" answered the sheep all together.

"Lambs?"

"He–aa–aa!" answered the lambs all together.

"Templeton?"

No answer.

"Templeton?"

No answer.

"Well, we are all here except the rat," said Charlotte. "I guess we can proceed without him. Now, all of you must have noticed what's been going on around here the last few days. The message I wrote in my web, praising Wilbur, has been received. The Zuckermans have fallen for it, and so has everybody else. Zuckerman thinks Wilbur is an unusual pig, and therefore he won't want to kill him and eat him. I dare say my trick will work and Wilbur's life can be saved."

How many animals does it sound like?

What animal is missing?

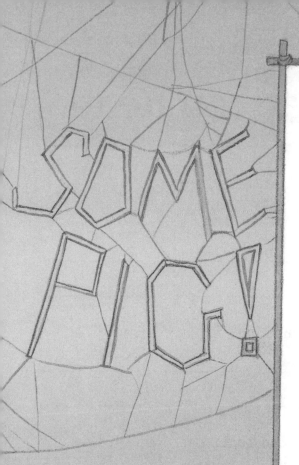

"Hurray!" cried everybody.

"Thank you very much," said Charlotte. "Now I called this meeting in order to get suggestions. I need new ideas for the web. People are already getting sick of reading the words 'Some Pig!' If anybody can think of another message, or remark, I'll be glad to weave it into the web. Any suggestions for a new slogan?"

"How about 'Pig Supreme'?" asked one of the lambs.

"No good," said Charlotte. "It sounds like a rich dessert."

"How about 'Terrific, terrific, terrific'?" asked the goose.

"Cut it down to one 'terrific' and it will do very nicely," said Charlotte. "I think 'terrific' might impress Zuckerman."

What does Wilbur say?

"But Charlotte," said Wilbur, "I'm *not* terrific."

"That doesn't make a particle of difference," replied Charlotte. "Not a particle. People believe almost everything they see in print. Does anybody know how to spell 'terrific'?"

Who knows how?

"I think," said the gander, "it's tee double ee double rr double rr double eye double ff double eye double see see see see see."

Thinking About What You Read

What did you find out?

1. Why did Charlotte write "Some Pig!" in her web?

_____

_____

2. What was the problem that made Charlotte call this meeting?

_____

_____

3. What slogan do you know about soft drinks, cars, or something else? Write it here.

_____

_____

_____

4. Why is "terrific" a good word for Charlotte to use in the new slogan?

_____

_____

_____

How did the author help you read the story?

Mr. White wanted his readers to enjoy this part of Wilbur's story. To do this, he tried to help his readers really *hear* the meeting that the animals have. He also wanted his readers to understand why some slogans work well for Wilbur while others don't.

1. Before writing the first part of this story, Mr. White probably visited a barnyard and listened to the sounds the animals made. So when he wrote the "words" that the gander, goose, and goslings say, he repeated them three times. Why?

_____

_____

2. What other animals usually make several sounds rather than just one? Write the name of the animal and the sounds each makes in the list below. I did one to get you started.

ANIMAL	SOUNDS
bee	*buzz, buzz, buzz*

3. Now try this. Reread the first part of Mr. White's story to yourself. Use the animals and sounds from your list in place of those Mr. White used. Do your animal names and sounds seem funny, too? Why do you think this is true?

4. Now let's look at how Mr. White told his readers about the slogans that were suggested. The first slogan that Mr. White wrote was "Some Pig!" Why is this a good slogan for Wilbur?

5. The next slogan that is suggested (by one of the lambs) is "Pig Supreme." Mr. White then tells his readers that Charlotte didn't like this slogan. Why didn't she like it?

6. If "Pig Supreme" were a rich meat dish, what things might be in it?

We certainly wouldn't want Wilbur to sound too delicious! Mr. White didn't want this, either. So the slogan "Pig Supreme" was not chosen. Slogans are tricky things. You have to be careful when you use them.

How can you use slogans to tell readers a message?

Think about Wilbur and Charlotte. Think about the reason all the animals were called to this meeting. Then make two bumper stickers in the space below. Make one for Wilbur and another for Charlotte. Draw pictures for your bumper stickers and try to write really good slogans for them.

Getting Ready to Read

1. At the beginning of this unit, you made a word web of things that make most people laugh. What are some of the things that make *you* laugh? Make another word web to list the things you think are funny.

things that make me laugh

I'll bet one of the first ideas you wrote was "comics," wasn't it? (If you didn't write "comics," go back and add it now.)

2. What comics or comic strips do you like best? List four titles here.

_____   _____

_____   _____

3. Choose one of the four comics you listed and tell why you like it in 25 words or less.

_____

_____

_____

4. If you have looked at the next page, you already know you are going to read some Garfield comics. What do you expect to read when you read about Garfield?

_____

_____

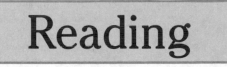

OK, you don't have to wait any longer. Go ahead and read the Garfield comics on pages 92 and 93, laughing all the way.

Thinking About What You Read

What did you find out?

1. What were three things Garfield didn't like?

_____

_____

2. What were two ways Jon, Garfield's owner, used to get Garfield to do what he wanted?

_____

_____

3. What are some ways that Garfield is like a real cat?

_____

_____

_____

4. What are some ways that Garfield is <u>not</u> like a real cat?

_____

_____

_____

How did the author help you read the comic strips?

Cartoonists don't have the space to use as many words as other writers do. So when you read any comic strip, you can expect to see **cartoon frames** and **dialogue balloons.** The frames, or individual pictures, show readers step-by-step what is happening. The dialogue balloons tell readers what the characters say and think.

1. Look at the second comic strip on page 93. How many steps does Mr. Davis use to tell what happened? And what do these individual frames or pictures show readers?

_____

_____

2. Now look at the comic strip on page 92. In this strip, Mr. Davis helps readers understand both what Jon is saying and what Garfield is thinking. He does this by using two different ways of drawing the dialogue balloons. Trace Jon's word balloons with a brown crayon and Garfield's with an orange crayon.

3. Mr. Davis also uses changes in the style of his letters to tell readers how the characters are feeling. Look at the comic strip on page 92 again. Find a frame where Mr. Davis wants his readers to know Jon is speaking sweetly. Circle the symbols Mr. Davis uses to tell readers this. Use a yellow crayon.

4. In the same comic strip, find a place where Mr. Davis wants his readers to know Garfield is surprised. Circle the words Mr. Davis wrote with a red crayon.

5. Look at the first comic strip on page 93. What way of drawing letters does Mr. Davis use here to tell his readers how Jon is feeling?

_____

_____

_____

How can you use cartoon frames, dialogue balloons, and different styles of letters to create your own comics?

Use the space below to draw and write a joke you know in comic strip style. Remember to use cartoon frames to show each part of what is happening and dialogue balloons to hold what your characters say. If you need to, use different styles of writing the words to tell readers how the characters are feeling.

That was easy, wasn't it?

Of course, one of the reasons Garfield comics are funny is because Mr. Davis draws Garfield in such a way that he looks funny. Draw a cartoon animal of your own. Then create a comic strip about your animal. Share your work with a friend.

Getting Ready to Read

1. Many people like to have something to eat just before they go to bed. What are four things you like to eat at that time?

   ☆ _____   ☆ _____

   ☆ _____   ☆ _____

2. You probably know that people sometimes eat unusual foods. Some people eat (and like) chocolate covered ants or grasshoppers. What are some other unusual foods that you know people eat?

   _____

3. What are two reasons why people might eat unusual foods?

   _____

   _____

4. If you really ate ants, grasshoppers, or the other things you listed, what might happen to you?

   _____

5. The title of the story you are going to read is *How to Eat Fried Worms*. What do you think you will find out as you read it?

   _____

6. What reasons might I have for putting this story in a unit called *LAUGHING ALL THE WAY?*

See if you are right. Read the story that begins on page 98. Answer the questions beside the story while you read.

How to Eat Fried Worms

by
Thomas Rockwell

His mother reached out and switched on the light. "What kind of pain, Billy?"

He stood beside the bed, clutching his stomach. "In my stomach. Oooo, there it goes again, I think."

"Did you eat something before bed?"

What had Billy eaten?

How many did he eat?

Why did this happen?

She was pulling on her bathrobe. "John, John." She shook her husband's shoulder.

He mumbled sleepily. "Did you eat candy or something before bed, Billy?"

"Worms," groaned Billy.

"*Worms?* John! John! Billy, what kind of worms?"

"Regular worms, night crawlers."

She felt his forehead, lifted his chin to look in his face. "You don't have a temperature. How many worms did you eat?"

"Five. Two boiled and three fried. With ketchup, mustard, horseradish, salt, pepper, butter. To make them taste better."

"Fried? Ketchup? Taste better? John! Wake up."

"I had this bet with Alan. Ohhhh." He groaned again.

"Take your hands away. Where does it hurt now? Show me."

What does Billy think might happen?

What is Billy to do?

"It doesn't really hurt so much now. It's just rumbling and gurgling something awful. It's—"

"Then why are you groaning?" asked his father, sitting up.

"Because I'm afraid it's going to *start* hurting. Do you think I'm going to die, Daddy?"

"Worms?" his father asked. "Ordinary worms? Earthworms?"

Billy nodded. "And how many did you eat this evening?"

"One this afternoon. I've eaten one every day for the last five days. But they weren't little ones; they were night crawlers, huge ones, as big as snakes almost."

His father lay back down, pulling the covers up around his shoulders. "Don't worry. Eating one night crawler a day for *six weeks* wouldn't hurt you. Go back to bed. It's probably all the ketchup and mustard that's upsetting your stomach. Drink a glass of warm water."

"John, are you sure?" asked Billy's mother. "It doesn't seem to me that worms could be a very healthy thing to eat, John?"

His father snuggled deeper under the covers. "I didn't say eating worms would turn him into an All-American fullback. I just said they wouldn't hurt him. Now let's go to sleep."

Thinking About What You Read

What did you find out?

1. Billy cooked his worms by boiling them and frying them. What are two other ways he could have cooked the worms?

☆ _____   ☆ _____

2. Billy put lots of stuff on the worms before he ate them. How do you think the worms would have tasted without the ketchup, mustard, and other things?

_____

_____

3. What bet would you take that would make you eat one worm a day for five days?

_____

_____

_____

_____

4. Did this story make you laugh? Here are some reasons why it might be funny to most people. Read them and put a number **1** beside the reason you think is best. Put a number **2** beside the reason you think is second best.

_____ Readers are surprised that Billy really ate worms.

_____ Readers know someone who ate something silly, like worms.

_____ Readers know no one would really eat worms, but the idea is so ridiculous, it's funny.

Now tell why you made your number one choice.

_____

_____

_____

_____

How did the author help you read the story?

Stories are very often funny or interesting because the author makes the characters so real that readers can almost see and hear what is going on. In this story, Mr. Rockwell helps his readers "see" by telling exactly what his characters **do.** Then he helps his readers "hear" by using a lot of **dialogue,** that is, the exact words the characters are saying.

1. Let's look back at the first part of the story to find the first two actions that Mr. Rockwell tells you Billy's mother did. Underline the words with a red crayon.

   Did you underline *reached* and *switched?* Good.

   Now read a little further and find four more actions Billy's mom did. Underline these actions with red, too.

2. What did you see Billy do in this part of the story? Use a green crayon to underline the words that tell you his actions after he woke his mom.

3. Now find the words that tell what Billy's father did. Mark these words with a blue crayon.

   All the words that you just underlined are **verbs.** They help you and other readers see what characters do.

4. Now let's see how Mr. Rockwell used dialogue to make this story sound real. He used words like *said* and *asked* to tell his readers who is talking. But Mr. Rockwell doesn't always do this. He knows that you know a **new paragraph** begins every time the speaker changes. He counts on you to be able to tell who is speaking by looking at what they are saying.

   Reread the story and draw colored arrows beside each new paragraph to show which person is speaking. Use a red arrow for Billy's mother, a green arrow for Billy, and a blue arrow for Billy's dad.

5. After you have the parts marked, ask two friends to help you read the story out loud. The colored arrows will help your friends know when to read their parts. Have your friends act out the parts, too. Tell them to watch for the underlined verbs that show the character's actions.

How can you use words and paragraphs to tell the actions characters do and the words they speak?

In this part of the story, Billy's dad is ready to go back to sleep. But Billy's mother and Billy are still worried. Write what these three people might do and say next in the story. Remember to use action words and new paragraphs to show when a different character is speaking.

Getting Ready to Read

Ebenezer Never-Could-Sneezer was an old French soldier. He had served in Napoleon's army. Now, I've heard that this Ebenezer could do *anything*. One thing he did very well was tell stories. He could tell stories by the hour.

But there was one thing Ebenezer could not do. He simply could not sneeze.

1. What are three things that can make people sneeze?

☆ _____

☆ _____

☆ _____

2. What might be two reasons why Ebenezer couldn't sneeze?

☆ _____

☆ _____

Well, the real reason Ebenezer couldn't sneeze is a simple one. He couldn't sneeze because he didn't have a nose, or so the story goes. Ebenezer lost his nose in a battle. A cannon took it away.

Sometimes Ebenezer wanted to sneeze. He'd catch a cold, or he'd feel his nose itching. But all Ebenezer could do was say, "Ah-ah-ah," or "Ker-ker-ker."

3. What might Ebenezer do to get a nose?

_____

_____

Poor Ebenezer needs help, you say? Well, read the story that begins on page 105 and see how he got it. Answer the questions beside the story as you read.

Ebenezer Never~Could~Sneezer

by Phyllis R. Fenner

What was new?

The new station shone like a dandelion in its fresh coat of yellow paint. The new tracks disappeared in one direction toward Paris and in the other direction toward the sea. The people were so excited that half of them were talking and half of them were laughing. Then the half that had been talking began to laugh and the half that had been laughing began to talk, until they were so mixed up that every one was talking out of one side of his mouth and laughing out of the other side of his mouth at the same time. You never heard such a bedlam! In the midst of it the town hall clock struck eleven. The train was due.

"H-oooooooo—h-ooooooooo-hoo-hoo!" Right on the dot the train whistled. Right on the dot it appeared in sight. Right on the dot it drew up at the station, bell ringing, steam escaping, engine panting, brakes grinding. Everybody shouted. Babies screamed and dogs barked. People waved from the windows of the train. People waved from everywhere on the station platform. Ebenezer waved both hands at once. "Rat-tat-tat" down the steps of the car came the Conductor's heels with the Conductor after them, throwing out his swelling chest as he came. He bowed. He beamed. He strutted. He shook hands with the Station Agent. He shook hands with the Mayor. He shook hands with the Mayor's new cane. He shook hands with everybody, including Ebenezer, until it was time for the train to depart.

What happened?

What happened?

Oh, that was a big moment for Ebenezer! Just as the Conductor shouted "A-llllll aboard!", just as the engine bell began to ring, just as the Engineer put his hand on the throttle, Ebenezer felt a sneeze coming. Back flew his head. Open flew his mouth. Tight shut his eyes. "Ah—ah—ah—," said Ebenezer. "CHOO!" said the engine. "Ker—ker—ker—," said Ebenezer. "CHOO!" said the engine. Oh it was a great big whacker of a choo, a delicious choo, the noisiest, juiciest CHOO you ever heard. "Ah—ah—ah—CHOO!" "Ker—ker—ker—CHOO!" The first good, satisfying sneeze Ebenezer had had since the battle of Austerlitz! He kept it up as long as the train was in sight.

From that day on, Ebenezer saved all his sneezes for train time. He knew when every train would depart and never missed a train. He would wait until the Conductor called, "A-llllll aboard!" He would wait until the engine bell rang and the Engineer put his hand on the throttle. Then he would throw back his head, open his mouth, shut his eyes and say, "Ah—ah—ah—" and "CHOO" would say the engine. "Ker—ker—ker—," he would say. "CHOO!" would say the engine. "Ah—ah—ah—choo—choo! Ker—ker—ker—choo—choo! Ah–ah–ker–choo–choo–choo! Ah-ker-choo–choo–choo! Ah–ker–choo–choo! Ah-ker-choo! Ah-ker-choo! Ah-ker-choo! Ahkerchoo, ahkerchoo, ahkerchoo-ahkerchoo-ahkerchoo-ahkerchoo!

There, now if you have your breath again after all that sneezing, here's the end of it. To this very day when the little boys and girls in that village hear the trains leaving the station, they laugh and say, "There goes Ebenezer-Never-Could-Sneezer's Nose."

Thinking About What You Read

What did you find out?

1. Why was Ebenezer at the train station?

_____

_____

_____

2. What was funny about the way the Conductor got off the train?

_____

_____

_____

3. What was funny about the way the Conductor acted at the station?

_____

_____

_____

4. What threc steps did Ebenezer take whenever he wanted to sneeze?

☆ _____

☆ _____

☆ _____

5. If you told this story, what would you probably do when you got to the end? Why?

_____

_____

_____

_____

How did the author help you read the story?

Ms. Fenner probably had a great time writing this story. Just reading it makes me laugh and laugh.

1. One of the things that makes me laugh is the picture Ms. Fenner paints when she tells what the crowd did at the station. Reread the first paragraph and draw a box around the part that tells what the crowd did. Then draw a picture below of how the people's faces would look.

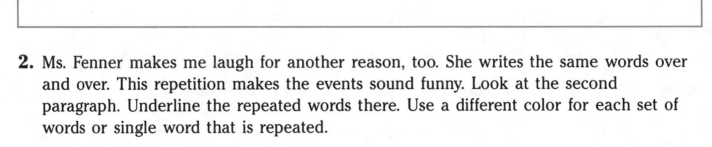

2. Ms. Fenner makes me laugh for another reason, too. She writes the same words over and over. This repetition makes the events sound funny. Look at the second paragraph. Underline the repeated words there. Use a different color for each set of words or single word that is repeated.

3. Ms. Fenner really makes me laugh when she tells about how Ebenezer did his sneezes. The repeated *ah*'s, *ker*'s, and *choo*'s only make the story sillier. I really wonder if anyone can tell the ending of this story without folding into a heap of laughter. Count the number of times Ebenezer sneezes in the next to the last paragraph. (Hint: use a colored crayon or marking pen to help you.) How many sneezes did you count?

_____

4. Look at that same paragraph again. What is one more way Ms. Fenner writes the sneezes to help make this story so funny?

_____

_____

How can you use repetition to tell a story?

1. Think of some sounds that you hear every day. Which ones might be funny when they are repeated? I started a list for you. Add three more sounds to it.

   ☆ *the dripping of a faucet or shower that gets faster and faster*

   ☆ _____

   ☆ _____

   ☆ _____

2. What are some problems people might have that could be connected with the sounds you just listed? I wrote an idea for my sound. Add an idea to the list for each of your sounds.

   ☆ *someone with a stuffy nose*

   ☆ _____

   ☆ _____

   ☆ _____

3. Choose one of the ideas from each list and write a silly story that uses repetition. There is space for your writing on this page and the next one. Remember, repeated words can tell about actions and things other than sounds. When you are done, share your silly story with a friend.

   _____

   _____

   _____

   _____

   _____

   _____

   _____

   _____

   _____

   _____